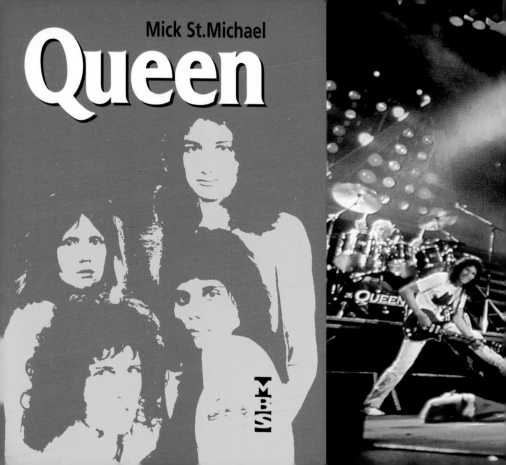

A MUSIC BOOK SERVICES PAPERBACK

This is a Carlton Book
Exclusively distributed in the U.S.A. by MBS Corporation,
16295 N.W. 13th Ave., Ste. B, Miami, Florida 33169

ISBN: 1 886894 27 2

Printed in Italy

THE AUTHOR
Mick St.Michael
A one-time guitarist, his previous work has included books on the Police,
Elvis Costello and James Dean. He lives in Hampshire with his family and CD collection.

# Contents

Introduction ............................................................6

Chapter 1. Smiling to stardom................................8

Chapter 2. Rock and rhapsodies............................36

Chapter 3. We are the champions..........................56

Chapter 4. Live Aid and after................................74

Chapter 5. The legend lives on............................104

Discography ........................................................112

Chronology..........................................................118

Index ..................................................................119

# Introduction

**T**he history of modern rock music is littered with powerful performers and showmen groups, yet few have retained a magnetic hold on audiences for as long as Queen. It requires all ingredients to work most of the time to sustain the kind of flamboyance Queen have exhibited throughout the life of the band without palling in the eyes of fans—and Queen have consistently got it right.

Glam Rock isn't enough, the appearance and presentation still needs good music for a group to survive. Queen's has been a combination of rich sounds, strong lyrics, nostalgia, pain, loneliness, angst and anger, party-time fun, sex 'n' sleaze; ranging from hard rock to full-blown opera, it's also been presented with a flair for show biz razzamatazz rarely seen before, often copied, never matched.

Although everyone in the band contributed to its success, it's the larger-than-life persona of Freddie Mercury that everyone remembers. From the very risqué name (for the early Seventies), Queen, Freddie has played with camp imagery, gender-bending and gay sensibility with the flair of a master juggler, transcending popular prejudices to appeal to an enormously wide audience. Freddie Mercury, Brian May, Roger Taylor and John Deacon—Queen—have been unique.

The band ended the day Freddie died of AIDS in November 1991, only a day after informing a shocked world that he was terminally ill. It was fitting that just three months later, the audience at the Brit Awards ceremony—Britain's equivalent of the Grammy Awards—should witness Brian May and Roger Taylor receive the award for Best British Single for 'These Are The Days Of Our Lives'.

Two years later, a UK Number 1 single—'Living On My Own'—reflected the fact that the music of Queen and their lead singer was still a staple of the 'classic rock' radio format. Beatboxes, rap and techno might claim their 15 minutes of fame, but it was clear Queen would retain their special and enduring place in the hearts of the world for as long as rock was played.

# Smiling to stardom

The Queen story inevitably starts with the inimitable Freddie Mercury. Born Frederick Bulsara on September 5, 1946, on the exotic island of Zanzibar (now part of Tanzania) off the coast of East Africa, Freddie was the son of a diplomat. At the

**Living up to a reputation for being serious.**

time, Africa provided few schools considered suitable for the education of expatriates, and so his early life was spent away from the family at boarding school—in this case in Bombay. It's a period of his life Freddie later looked back on with little amusement.

"You had to do what you were told, so the sensible thing was to make the most of it," he said. "I grew up very quickly. All the things they say about [boarding schools] is more or less true. All the bullying and everything else. I've had the odd schoolmaster chasing me. It didn't shock me because somehow boarding schools... you're not confronted by it, you are just slowly aware of it. It's going through life."

At 13 he came to Britain with his parents, Bomi and Jer, to complete his schooling, at which point he opted for the life of an art student—a course of action followed by many Sixties' pop stars in the apparent belief that art college informality left plenty of time for rehearsals. The Ealing School of Art in West London boasted Rolling Stone Ron Wood and Who mainman Pete Townshend among its former pupils—and Freddie was more than happy to follow in their footsteps.

Unlike several famous names who went the art student route, he graduated with a diploma in art and design, and felt the Ealing years were an early ingredient of his success. "Art school teaches you to be more fashion-conscious, to be always one step ahead," he later opined. But music rivalled his love of design and he took his first steps to stardom with two local outfits—Sour Milk Sea and Wreckage.

## Smiling through

It was the late Sixties and a hard, raw sound was developing, exemplified by the music of Jimi Hendrix and Cream. Freddie loved the power of hard rock but also enjoyed the harmonic Beach Boys, too. He harboured a dream to combine both, and in 1970 his wish came true. Discover-

**Freddie in the mid-Seventies.**

**Brian May defined the Queen guitar sound.**

ing a talent for songwriting, he re-invented himself: as Freddie Mercury, messenger of the gods, he ventured forth into the pop world... and fate gave him a Smile.

Roger Taylor, a young Rod Stewart lookalike and biology student, teamed up with Freddie to run a clothes stall at London's fashionable Kensington Market. Roger also played drums with a students' band called Smile, which is how Freddie was introduced to his future Queen bandmates. Brian May, a science student, played a guitar he'd fashioned from the parts of an old fireplace. May lived only yards away from Freddie but they had never met.

Smile's bass player and vocalist, Tim Staffell, who also attended Ealing School of Art, had

> "We travelled around the country a fair bit, as far as Cornwall and Liverpool, and although we did well in some places, we never felt we were getting anywhere."
> *Brian May*

played with May in a school band, performing an odd mix of covers from the Everly Brothers and Buddy Holly, rubbing shoulders with James Brown and Eddie Floyd's soul. Later they graduated to Rolling Stones and Yardbirds-style R&B, but the ambitious Brian eventually left because he wanted to do something more original.

He met Roger Taylor after advertising on a notice board at college for a drummer and they formed Smile. "We travelled around the country a fair bit, as far as Cornwall and Liverpool, and although we did well in some places, we never felt we were getting anywhere," said Brian, "because if you don't have a record out, people tend to forget who you are very quickly."

## Open to interpretation

Smile did get a contract—with the Mercury label—and recorded some six tracks, but a single in America was their only release. Tim Staffell decided that he'd had enough and Freddie saw his chance.

He greeted his future colleagues with the refreshing directness they would come to know as his trademark: "Why are you wasting your time doing this? You should do more original material. You should be more demonstrative in the way that you put the music across. If I was your singer, that's what I'd be doing!" Freddie was in.

His directness went further. He came up with

**The group together promoting** *Innuendo.*

**Above: Roger Taylor lost in the crowd.**

**Right: Brian May stands in full battle dress.**

the name for the new group: Queen. "It's just a name, but it's very regal, obviously, and it sounds splendid," said Freddie, disingenuously. "It's a strong name, very universal and immediate. It had a lot of visual potential and was open to all sorts of interpretations. I was certainly aware of the gay connotations, but that was just one facet of it."

Freddie's personal life was also "open to interpretation", though at first his gayness wasn't apparent. He'd started living with Mary Austin—manageress of the Biba boutique, just across the road from his and Roger Taylor's Kensington Market stall—whom he would later describe as his "common-law wife". Later, his bisexual lifestyle mutated their relationship into a brother-sister one.

Queen didn't rush into success. Throughout 1970, the group rehearsed and wrote songs, occasionally testing the water by playing at friends' parties. Bass players came and went till electronics student John Deacon plugged in to complete the line-up.

"We just knew he was the right one," said

Brian, "even though he was so quiet. He hardly spoke to us at all." That's probably because he wasn't as sure of Queen as they were of him. "I was possibly the one person in the group who could look at it from the outside, because I came in as the fourth person in the band," he said later. "I knew there was something there but I wasn't convinced of it... until possibly the *Sheer Heart Attack* album." That was, of course, some years away.

In musical terms, Queen's four members found common ground in heavy rock. Freddie liked rock, too, but despaired at supergroups

**John Deacon shows off Seventies fashion.**

"I was possibly the one person in the group who could look at it from the outside, because I came in as the fourth person in the band."
*John Deacon*

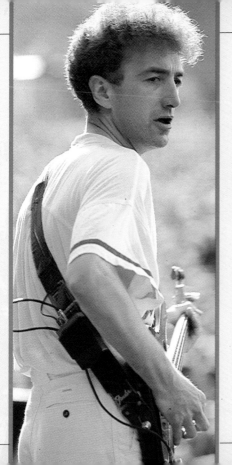

like Deep Purple and Led Zeppelin, whose idea of stage dress was brocade waistcoats and the occasional loon pant among the wall-to-wall denim. Long before pop video, he realised powerful rock and theatrics could mix to create music that was not only great listening but also good viewing. Elsewhere, David Bowie was working along similar lines; it was no coincidence that Queen and Bowie later got together to cut the UK Number 1 single 'Under Pressure'.

## Cecil B De Mille of rock

Smile had been a lot of hard work for little reward: now Freddie was pointing the way to the promised land... if Brian, John and Roger had the guts to follow. And guts were needed: "When I look back on all that black varnish, chiffon, satin and that," Freddie later admitted, "I think, God, what was I doing?"

Queen discovered a trademark by accident when playing a low-key gig at a girls' school. The bottom fell off Freddie's mike-stand halfway through the performance, and he decided he

**Less hair and less flares—John in the Eighties.**

**Mott the Hoople—early Queen tour mates.**

liked it. A tour of Cornwall, in South West England, during the holiday season followed, but an unknown band couldn't always pull the crowd: just six people turned up at one venue!

Their strength was their attitude: each did what they were best at. John organized gigs, art student Freddie was pressed into service designing the distinctive Queen crest. Even at that time, his designs were on a grand camp scale: "We'll be the Cecil B De Mille of rock! Always wanting to do things bigger and better."

Brian agreed: "Freddie always looked like a

star and acted like a star even though he was penniless. When we started sharing a flat, Fred would bring home these great bags of stuff, pull out some horrible strip of cloth and say, 'Look at this beautiful garment! This is going to fetch a fortune'!"

In 1971, world domination plans proceeded apace. Their stage act mixed original material with rock classics, from artists such as Elvis Presley's 'Jailhouse Rock' and Bo Diddley's 'I'm A Man'. "If you go on stage and people don't know your material," Brian explained, "you can get boring if you do your own stuff all the time. You can only get so far in playing to audiences who don't understand what you're doing, so we did more heavy rock 'n' roll, with the Queen delivery, to give people something they could get hold of—get on, sock it to 'em, get off!" Not a bad slogan.

## No rags to riches

Despite some success, the group stubbornly held on to their day jobs and academic studies. It was slow going, but Roger had faith that Queen would soon amount to something. "For the first

**Mr Taylor is caught in a thoughtful moment.**

> **"We'll be the Cecil B De Mille of rock! Always wanting to do things bigger and better."**
> *Freddie Mercury*

two years, nothing really happened. We were all studying, but progress in the band was nil. We had great ideas, though, and somehow I think we all felt we'd get through."

Brian agreed. "If we were going to drop the careers we'd trained hard for, we wanted to make a really good job of music. We all had quite a bit to lose, really, and it didn't come easy. To be honest, I don't think any of us realized it would take a full three years to get anywhere. It was certainly no fairy tale."

**Eyecatching, even in early shots.**

**Brian and his homemade guitar.**

**A right Royal Freddie struts his regal stuff.**

Queen made demo tapes early in 1972, at London's De Lane Lea Studios, where they were spotted by producer Roy Thomas Baker, the man who would produce their first four albums. The tapes were of such good quality that one track—'The Night Comes Down'—later appeared on the band's first album in unchanged form. Impressed, Baker set up a November gig at the Pheasantry club in London's trendy Kings Road as an audition for his bosses to see Queen. It went well, and the first months of 1973 were spent at London's Trident studios recording their first album, called simply—but "regally"—*Queen*.

They took a break from sessions in April to play at London's legendary Marquee Club, inspiring rave reviews in the music press—even though they were months from releasing anything on disc. During the long wait for the album, Queen released a cover version of the Beach Boys number, 'I Can Hear Music'.

"Robin Cable, who we also knew in Trident Studios, was doing a recreation of the Phil Spector sound," said Brian "and was very keen for

...asting success—the band laid-back and relaxed for champagne in Japan.

Freddie to be vocalist. Once Freddie was in there, he suggested that it should have some of my guitar work in this instrumental space they'd left blank.

"They also used Roger to do some percussion

**Brian May with fellow "axe" hero Jeff Beck.**

overdubs, like the maraccas and tambourines, which is a part of the Phil Spector sound. I like that quite a lot, and I thought it was a good piece of work."

'I Can Hear Music' wasn't released as a Queen single but under the name of Larry Lurex (a lampoon on the then-popular Gary Glitter). It failed

to sell and is consequently very rare.

### The first album

*Queen* was finally released in July 1973 and credited an unknown name among the musicians: Deacon John on bass! "We used to call him Deacon John," explained Brian, "and it appeared like that on the first album. But after that, he objected to it, and said he wanted to be called John Deacon. I don't really know why we called him Deacon John in the first place—just one of those silly things."

Brian May's guitar conjured up sounds which it was felt many people might confuse with syn-

thesizers, so the band decided to clarify matters and put a "No synthesizers" note on the sleeve.

"We wanted to make sure people knew it was all guitars and voices," he insisted, "and that stuck with us for a long time. I think that for the first nine albums we made, there was

*Queen* **launched on an unsuspecting world.**

> "For the first two years, nothing really happened. We were all studying, but progress in the band was nil. We had great ideas, though and somehow I think we all felt we'd get through."
> *Roger Taylor*

**Ian Hunter, from Mott the Hoople, mid-song.**

never a synthesizer and never an orchestra, never any other player except us on the records."

Freddie's first recorded tour de force was undoubtedly 'My Fairy King', with its use of piano. A self-taught pianist, he hadn't played on-stage, so the studio was the first time the trademark Queen sound of contrasting piano and guitar was heard. And it was a sound with possibilities: adding multiple voice overdubs and harmonies would, in 1974, lead to 'The March Of The Black Queen' on the second album, then 'Bohemian Rhapsody' later.

Eclectically, a Led Zeppelin influence could be heard—in 'Father To Son'—as could touches of The Who, and it was clear that Queen saw themselves as cast in this classic British rock mould. Yet it fell to 'Keep Yourself Alive', with its characteristic overdriven guitar sound, to be the band's first official single.

## Wear and tear

Now acclaimed as a classic, 'Keep Yourself Alive' was rejected no fewer than five times by BBC's Radio 1 playlist panel—so instead of promoting

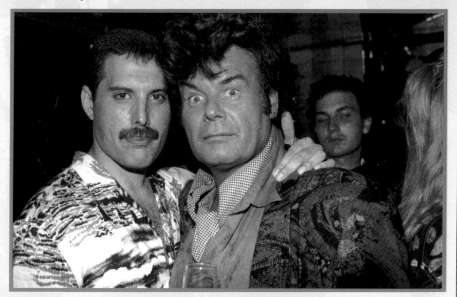

**Freddie 'n' Gary, the Queen and King of glam.**

the album, the band disappeared with Roy Baker to cut *Queen II* during August 1973. When the BBC finally saw the light and relented, Queen recorded their first Radio 1 session for *Sounds Of* *The Seventies.*

It's indicative of a common sense attitude that despite their newly-acquired fame, Brian still felt the need to start a part-time teaching job in Stockwell, South London, to keep money coming in. November and December 1973 were

**From the third album, *Sheer Heart Attack*.**

spent touring Britain as special guests of Bowie protégés Mott The Hoople, whose fans were taken aback by Freddie's latest fashion discovery... black nail varnish!

"The opportunity of playing with Mott was great," admitted a confident Freddie, "but I knew damn well the moment we finished that tour, as far as Britain was concerned, we'd be headlining." And so it proved.

Queen started the new year of 1974 with

> "We were trying to push studio techniques to a new limit for rock groups, and we wore the tape literally to the point where you could see through it, because we were doing so many overdubs."
> *Brian May*

sunshine, by flying to Melbourne, Australia, for a music festival in February—the same month as their first chart single, 'Seven Seas Of Rhye', was released. It reached Number 10 in the UK, setting the stage for the March release of *Queen II*. If much of the first album had been tried and tested live, *Queen II* was emphatically a studio creation, most of which was too complicated for a four-piece outfit to play on stage.

"We were trying to push studio techniques to a new limit for rock groups," explained Brian, "and we wore the tape literally to the point where you could see through it, because we

**Understating as ever, for that Oriental look.**

were doing so many overdubs. We were building up 50-piece choir-type effects and loads of guitars to get this thick orchestra sound. In a way, it was going over the top... the second album was an adventure into the world of what can be done and hadn't been done before."

## Stateside nightmare

In fact its original title had been 'Over The Top', but it was with the more conventionally, though still regally titled *Queen II* that the band hit the road in March 1974 to promote their first headlining UK tour. And the following month they were off with Mott The Hoople again—this time on their first US concert tour.

Brian recalls it was something of an eye-opener. "I remember going to Los Angeles the first time (we were sold out a couple of nights in a small place), and I went to see Led Zeppelin at the Forum. If we can ever play here, that would be the ultimate dream come true, I thought."

But the reality was nightmarish. Brian fell ill and Queen returned home after just five dates.

**Brian May—a man, his guitar and a perm.**

"I felt really bad at having let the group down at such an important place, but there was nothing I could do about it. It was hepatitis, which I think you can get sometimes when you're emotionally run-down. And almost immediately after that, we were due to start recording *Sheer Heart Attack*."

Brian's illness dragged on, causing difficulties for the group in getting *Sheer Heart Attack* together, and their third LP ended up being recorded in no fewer than four studios between July and September. It was bad timing for a band that had broken but not yet made it big enough to be certain of continued success.

The struggle to get *Sheer Heart Attack* through proved to be worth it, however, when the 'Killer Queen' single made UK Number 2 in October. It was the turning point. Touring Britain for the third time in a year, the power of their live performances boosted the album to Number 2 in the UK. Queen had arrived!

## Classy whores

Several tracks of *Sheer Heart Attack* had been laid down before Brian May fell ill. When he

**An impassioned, operatic Freddie moment.**

rejoined them in the studio, they presented him with others, like Freddie's 'Flick Of The Wrist', which in turn energized him to write.

'Now I'm Here', inspired by memories of their American tour, was an especially memorable May composition, as was the echoing 'Brighton Rock', which soon became a stage favourite. The number's central solo section, which started life on the Mott The Hoople tour and gradually

**A content Japanese crowd on one of the later Queen tours.**

> **"We weren't going for hits, but we did think that perhaps we'd dished up a bit too much for people to swallow on *Queen II*."**
> **Brian May**

For their record company, *Sheer Heart Attack* put Queen on the music map with a vengeance. As often happens with breakthrough albums, its success with the public boosted interest in their previous releases, and by the time the group toured Japan in 1975, all four albums would

expanded, made novel and effective use of a repeat guitar phrase.

*Sheer Heart Attack* was direct, avoiding some of the fussiness of the earlier albums. "We weren't going for hits," Brian admitted, "but we did think that perhaps we'd dished up a bit too much for people to swallow on *Queen II*."

Lyrically, the new album showcased Freddie's fascination with class and sleaze. "'Killer Queen', he explained, "is about a high-class call girl. I'm trying to say that classy people can be whores too."

**Tickling the ivories and the vocal chords.**

**Modelling the latest off-the-shoulder leotard.**

have placings in the UK charts.

For Brian, success had happened not a moment too soon. " 'Killer Queen' was the turning point," he later reflected. "It was the song that best summed up our kind of music, and a big hit, and we desperately needed it as a mark of something successful happening for us."

## The American curse

Freddie found fame exhilarating and just the "teeniest" bit frightening. "I'm very emotional," he confessed. "Whereas before, I was given time to make my decisions, now nearly all of us are so highly strung we just snap. We always argue but I think that's a healthy sign because we get to the root of the matter and squeeze the best out. But lately so much is happening, it's escalating so fast that everybody wants to know almost instantly, and I certainly get very temperamental."

When Queen visited America for the second time, they were top of the bill. But the American curse struck again. Freddie lost his voice after the Washington concert on February 24, 1975,

In there somewhere, Queen performing at one of the early Hyde Park gigs in the Seventies.

**The legendary 'Bohemian Rhapsody' video.**

forcing the cancellation of several performances. Two weeks' rest and recuperation followed before the tour resumed. For Freddie, there was a consolation in receiving a British Ivor Novello Award for 'Killer Queen'.

In April, following a ten-day holiday in Hawaii, it was Japan's turn to encounter the Queen live experience. "In Japan something clicked," revealed Brian May. "When we went through customs into the airport lounge in Tokyo, there were 3,000 little girls screaming at us. Suddenly we were the Beatles. We literally had to be carried over the heads of these kids. I was half scared and half amused. This wasn't a rock band thing, this was being a teen idol. But we had to admit it was fun!"

With Freddie back in full voice after his break, the band played for broke, the fans loved them, and their fanatical Far East following dates from that tour.

**Right: Roger and Freddie getting together.**

# Rock and rhapsodies

Queen had happened in a big way, but more was to come when, on the last day of October 1975, they released 'Bohemian Rhapsody'. Within weeks, it would hit Number 1 in the UK, win Freddie his second Ivor Novello award and establish the phenomenon of the rock video.

Promotional films were nothing new. Unable—or unwilling—to appear on BBC Television's enduring *Top Of The Pops*, the Beatles had made a special film of themselves for the double-hit singles, 'Strawberry Fields Forever' and 'Penny Lane', in the mid-Sixties. Other artists since had followed suit, although most films were mundane, literal performances of singer or band on a film studio stage.

And most of them—unlike those of the Beatles—were intended as mere stand-ins for the real thing. Queen's video for 'Bohemian Rhapsody' was something quite else—a work of art. It was the first time that for many British TV fans, the stand-in was sufficient to replace the band itself, not better but different and equally exciting to watch.

The "four heads" image from the clip is the strongest of many associated with Queen, and has often been imitated or parodied. Yet the video itself was something of an afterthought to the song, filmed a month after the single's release. "At the time we were touring England," explained John, "and we knew we wouldn't be able to get to record *Top Of The Pops* on the Wednesday." The BBC programme's traditional broadcast day was Thursday, with studio recordings made the day before.

The video featured large facial close-ups of

**Live passion and energy—Roger and Freddie.**

the group, rapidly dissolving between them. The power of the resulting image, as is often the case with great ideas, came less from good judgment than necessity, as John admitted. "Our managers at the time had a mobile unit, so it was actually shot on video in about four hours!" With a budget of just £4,500 ($6,750), it was the scoop of the century!

## Operatic single

The album from which it was extracted, *A Night At The Opera*, became both a debut chart-topper and their first platinum album after its December release. But all reviews voted for 'Rhapsody', at 5 minutes, 52 seconds, among the longest UK Number 1 singles ever.

It established the single as a potential art form and not just another disposable pop tune. Nevertheless it was not universally admired. "A lot of people slammed 'Bohemian Rhapsody'," complained Freddie. "But who can you compare that to? Name one group that's done an operatic single."

Producer Roy Thomas Baker added his own recollections. "Freddie would walk in and say,

**Above: Roger watching Freddie's biker look.**

**Left: All wrapped up—the Harlequin look.**

'I've got some new ideas for the vocals—we'll stick some Galileos in here'. Then there were all the guitar overdubs and getting on for two days to mix it. I'd say that track, on its own, took getting on for three weeks, because it's three songs

**Lights, smoke and a pair of live Killers.**

merged together!"

After recording the track, even the flamboyant Freddie wondered if radio would take to their new single. To settle his doubts, he enlisted the help of BBC Radio One's zany disc jockey, Kenny Everett. "I remember him being so unsure about this piece of genius," recalled Everett. "It was very odd, when you look at it in retrospect, because it was so great." Later, of course, Freddie would be the last to admit anything but

> **"I remember him being so unsure about this piece of genius, it was very odd, when you look at it in retrospect, because it was so great."**
> *Kenny Everett*

a long time. It was prompted by a weird dream—not, the down-to-earth guitarist admitted, his usual inspiration for songwriting. 'Good Company' was even more remarkable—all the trumpets and clarinets were actually recreated by his guitar. "To get the effect of the instru-

**Ian Hunter entirely engrossed in his music.**

utter confidence in the track. "We were adamant that 'Bohemian Rhapsody' would be a hit in its entirety. We have been forced to make compromises, but cutting up a song will never be one of them."

### Slash to heavy rock

The band regarded *A Night At The Opera* as their masterpiece. Despite its title, it wasn't created overnight; they'd worked hard on it and it contained many future Queen classics.

May's 'The Prophet's Song' had been around

ments," he explained, "I was doing one note at a time with the pedal and building them up. So you can imagine how long it took! It was a bit of fun, but a semi-serious piece of work because so much time went into it."

The folksy '39' was played on-stage as an acoustic quartet, and Roger Taylor came out from behind the drumkit with a tambourine to weigh in vocally with the upbeat 'I'm In Love With My

**An unusually restrained early performance.**

Car', the hit single's B-side. "There was such a wide variety on those albums," Brian commented, "Fred doing a really quite slushy ballad, then a heavy rock thing, then something else—and we were willing to try everything because we always wanted to expand our range."

The second single from the album came, unusually, from the pen of John Deacon—'You're My Best Friend' coasted on a wash of electric piano from Freddie Mercury. From that time onward, keyboards would become standard stage kit, though backing tapes were required to reproduce 'Bohemian Rhapsody' even approximately—this was, after all, before the days of digital sampling.

The lyrics of '39' were inspired both by *The River*, a novel by Herman Hesse, and Brian's own travels round the world with a group that was becoming ever-more globally popular. Their best year yet, 1975, was rounded off in suitable style with a Christmas Eve show broadcast by BBC Television's "serious" music programme, the *Old Grey Whistle Test*, from London's Hammersmith Odeon.

> *"At one point two or three years after we began, we nearly disbanded. We felt it wasn't working, there were too many sharks in the business."*
> *Freddie Mercury*

## No lap of luxury

The new LP had gained Queen millions of new fans—yet Freddie's confident public face hid an inner uncertainty. "At one point two or three years after we began, we nearly disbanded," he later revealed. "We felt it wasn't working, there were too many sharks in the business and it was all getting too much for us. But something inside us kept us going, and we learned from our experiences, good and bad."

**Hide behind a disguise—could it be Freddie?**

The money would come, in time, but while Freddie could indulge expensive tastes on-stage with his peacock-like costumes, once the house lights went off after the show, the former second-hand clothes vendor was hardly returning to the lap of luxury. "We didn't make any money until *A Night At The Opera*. Most of our income was consumed by litigation and things like that."

They had, in fact, gone through several managers. One earned the memorable parting epithet: "Our old management is deceased. They cease to exist in any capacity with us whatsoever. One leaves them behind like one leaves excreta. We feel so relieved!"

While touring in America in February 1976, all but John sang on a solo album by Ian Hunter, former Mott The Hoople main man. It was a form of "thank you" for Hunter's support for them in providing exposure on earlier tours. And they followed America with Japan in March and Australia in April.

## Concert in the Park

The tour's September highlight was a triumphant return home to play a free gig in London's Hyde Park—an outdoor venue made popular by the Rolling Stones and Blind Faith, among others. "It was a real high," commented an awestruck Brian May, looking out on a sea of 150,000 adoring faces.

The Hyde Park concert ensured a high level

**Strumming along, oblivious to the world.**

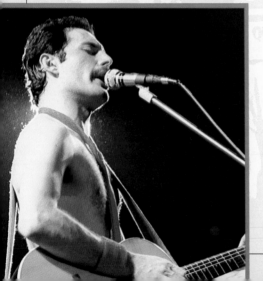

**Underneath all the glamour and the glitz, Freddie shows he's really just one of the crowd.**

of expectation for Queen's eagerly-awaited fifth album, *A Day At The Races*, and it notched up half a million advance orders in the UK before its December release, guaranteeing the UK Number 1 slot within the month. This was the first album Queen had produced without Roy Baker (who moved on to produce hits for the Cars and others), its sales helped along by the preceding single, 'Somebody To Love', which shot up the UK charts to Number 2.

In many respects, *A Day At The Races* could be considered *A Night At The Opera—Part II*, since the material for both albums was written around the same time. Predictably, the music press viewed *Races* as a distinct follow-up to *Opera*, when really it was an extension. Queen had intended no significant progression—fine for the fans, but critics found it harder to handle.

> **"I know it happens to everybody else as well, and it's a normal consequence of success in England — a lot of people resent your success."**
> *Brian May*

**Leather jacket, beer and microphone pout.**

That said, there was a superb Brian May rocker, 'Tie Your Mother Down', to release as a follow-up single, while Freddie's 'Good Old Fashioned Lover Boy' was high camp in—as equally camp DJ Kenny Everett's trademark slogan had it—the best possible taste.

Press reaction to Queen, never warm, now turned bitter, and the band reacted by declining interviews by anyone they considered might "stitch them up." "Our silence wasn't through choice," Brian May later insisted, "it was really having no one to talk to who was going to write anything which would be of any use to us. I know it happens to everybody else as well, and it's a normal consequence of success in England—a lot of people resent your success."

## Mister Ferocious

The arrival of the punk music culture in 1977 didn't help the ever-ready-to-move-on music press attitude. To new groups like the Damned and the Clash, Queen were archetypical of the glam end of "pomp rock"—they were the Establishment and everything punk stood against. Punk rock's first big year was coincidentally the

**Anguish and emotion in an early concert.**

> **"We were recording an album next door to the Sex Pistols, and one day Sid Vicious stumbled in and yelled at Freddie, "Ullo, Fred, so you've really brought ballet to the masses then?"**
> *Roger Taylor*

Silver Jubilee of Queen Elizabeth II, and while the Sex Pistols musically reviled the Queen of England, the other Queen were abroad, playing their biggest tour yet.

This eight month effort began in January, with up-and-coming Irish band Thin Lizzy in support, taking in the USA, Canada and Europe. During their absence, 'Bohemian Rhapsody' won a Brit award—the UK music industry's version of a Grammy—for the best single in 25 years.

**How they all looked in the early Eighties.**

"Brits" were not awards punk rockers would affect to notice, but according to Roger Taylor, some punks were closet fans.

"We were recording an album next door to the Sex Pistols, and one day [bassist] Sid Vicious stumbled in and yelled at Freddie, "Ullo, Fred, so you've really brought ballet to the masses then?' Freddie just turned round and said, 'Ah, Mr Ferocious. Well, we're trying our best, dear'!"

Exiled or not by press antipathy and the noisy new punk audience, Queen couldn't resist playing a couple of showpiece concerts in June at London's Earls Court. Organized as part of the official Jubilee celebrations, the cost of the one-off special effects ensured the band lost money on the night. It was patriotic, though. "I have a lot of respect for royalty," insisted Freddie, ensuring further revilement from punks but appealing to older fans.

## Anthemic "up yours"

Sessions for their next album, *News Of The World*, started in July, with a foretaste in the October release of 'We Are The Champions'.

**Glittering and dynamic, the focus of it all.**

> ## "I have a lot of respect for royalty."
> ### Freddie Mercury

**Live in the late Seventies, rocking away.**

Their American touring paid off, too, as 'We Are The Champions' reached Number 4 in the US Top 100, their best-selling American single so far, and it reached Number 2 in the UK charts. A typically flamboyant Freddie Mercury number, the anthemic chant was clearly meant as an autobiographical "up yours" to the critics, a hymn for the fans and altogether as loud and proud as the man himself.

Part of its success in Britain was undoubtedly due to its appeal to soccer fans. " 'We Are The Champions' has been taken up by football fans because it's a winners' song," explained Freddie. It might have been the A-side, but Brian May's

**The 'Bicycle Race' video—it was to be banned.**

equally anthemic B-side, 'We Will Rock You' would achieve just as much fame—most recently in the Nineties as theme tune to UK television's *Gladiators* game show.

*News Of The World*, however, had much more to offer as an album than mere bombast, including, intriguingly, a Taylor-penned track titled 'Sheer Heart Attack'. Having "done studios to death with the previous two albums," as Brian put it, there was a move afoot to go for

**Right: Joined by inflatable friends on bikes.**

something simpler and more direct.

May's 'Sleeping On The Sidewalk' was more or less written on the spot and recorded straight away—and though he modestly disclaimed it as "the sort of thing any guitarist who had played a bit of blues would do", it was a warm and slightly Claptonesque number. 'It's Late' was much closer to typical Queen, while John Deacon weighed in with a couple of compositions, including 'Spread Your Wings'.

*News Of The World* hit the UK shops in October, but only made Number 4, leading everybody but Queen and their fans to believe they were on the slide. It wasn't to be.

### An erotic interlude

From January to March, the European leg of the 1978 tour was recorded for eventual release as the double-album *Live Killers*, which reached Number 3 in the UK charts, disproving fears that

**Left: Drama in the original Flash Gordon.**

the group was losing its grip.

Opening with the chanting 'We Will Rock You', it ran through the repertoire from the old favourite 'Death On Two Legs'—though its typically cheeky Freddie intro had to be 'bleeped' by a worried record company—to 'Brighton Rock', which took up most of the third side, ending in style with 'We Are The Champions' and their own special version of 'God Save The Queen'.

One special highlight was Freddie's 'Get

**A rare picture of the band relaxing at home.**

Down, Make Love', where Brian used a harmoniser pedal to feed back on itself. Together with noises from Freddie, it became what the guitarist smilingly called "a sort of erotic interlude." The single was 'Love Of My Life', but like most live singles it didn't hit.

The same couldn't be said of their next release, 'Bicycle Race'/'Fat Bottomed Girls', a taster for a new studio album to be called *Jazz* and released in November 1978. The big news was that Queen had re-hired Roy Baker to co-produce it. "We thought it would be nice to try again with a producer on whom we could put some of the responsibility," commented Brian. "We'd found a few of our own methods, and so had he. And on top of what we'd collectively learned would mean there would be some new stuff going on. It worked pretty well."

The good tracks included 'Let Me Entertain You', which had been previewed in the live shows, and a strong second single in Freddie's typically flamboyant 'Don't Stop Me Now'.

**Ready for a *Hot Space* autograph session.**

Released as the band toured the States, *Jazz* was launched by a party in New Orleans featuring dwarves, magicians, jugglers and naked mud-wrestlers. It reached Number 2 in Britain and went Gold. The Midas touch had definitely returned.

# We are the champions!

The year 1980 was memorable, even for Queen. Noted film producer Dino de Laurentiis commissioned them to write the theme to his next blockbuster, adapted from the comic *Flash Gordon*, the soundtrack of which would be released in time for Christmas. 'Crazy Little Thing Called Love'—a song Freddie claimed he "wrote in the bath"—topped the US charts. And on December 26 a concert at London's Hammersmith Odeon was recorded as a fund-raiser for the people of war-torn Kampuchea, ending the year in fine style.

First into the record shops was *The Game* in June, which made a welcome return to the top of the UK album charts and went Gold. The band looked suitably macho on the cover, dressed in leather jackets, but the biggest change in musical approach was that Queen had finally discovered synthesizers.

Freddie, in particular, thought previous albums had been almost too diverse, so *The Game* was deliberately purposeful, riding on rhythm and sparingly played—a manifesto for the Eighties to come. The synthesizers came from working on 'Flash Gordon' at the same time and, as Brian explained, the catalyst was Roger.

**More frolics from 'I Want To Break Free'.**

"He had this OBX [synthesizer] which he was playing around with, which obviously produced some good sounds. Synths had advanced an awful long way since those early days," he continued, but insisted there was "no danger of the synth taking over. I would never allow that to happen—although I'm much happier using them than I used to be."

### Flash Gordon approaching

'Crazy Little Thing Called Love' had an almost rockabilly feel, with Brian abandoning his beloved home-made guitar for a twangy, country-flavoured Fender Telecaster, which he'd never used on record before. "It was done with Elvis Presley in mind, obviously—I thought Freddie sounded a bit like Elvis."

Another 'Champions'-style sports theme was created in 'Another One Bites The Dust', a rare John Deacon A-side that gave the band chart success in both Britain and the US. The Americans took to the track's black funk feel, a first for Queen, and made it their second US Number

**Busy day—a megastar's work is never done.**

**Crown in hand, the lord of all he surveys.**

1. To reciprocate, Queen toured America for three months.

Then came the year's second release. *Flash Gordon—The Original Soundtrack*, produced by Brian May, reached Number 10 in the UK album charts—coincidentally, the same position as the title-track single. "We were given the licence to do what we liked," commented Brian, and the result more than stood up in its own right.

Queen had been asked to write for film soundtracks before but turned them down. "This one was different in that it was a proper film and had a real story, which wasn't based around music," explained May. "We would be writing a film score in the way anyone else writes a film

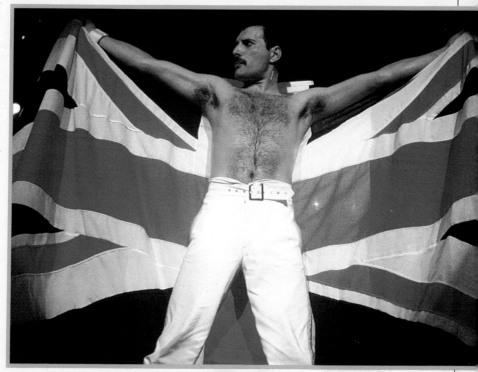

**Ever the loyal patriot, wrapped in the British flag.**

score, which is basically background music, but can obviously help the film if it's strong enough. That was the attraction."

The soundtrack album was released in December 1980, at which point Queen had sold over 45 million records worldwide.

## The Latin lovers

A step into uncharted rock territory was taken in February 1981 with the first ever stadium rock tour of South America. Exotically-born Freddie found Latin flamboyance an instant attraction. It was evidently mutual—their first visits to Argentina and Brazil attracted half a million to only eight concerts, and the public put every Queen album into the national Top 10 charts.

Equipment for the shows had to be transported from the US and Japan, so it was an expensive business, but the world's biggest-ever paying audience—251,000 at Sao Paulo's Morumbi Stadium—made it all worthwhile. "We were really nervous," admitted Freddie in a rare public show of anxiety. "We had no right to automatically expect the works from an alien territory. I don't think they'd ever seen such an ambitious show, with this lighting and effects." He needn't have worried.

More off the beaten rock 'n' roll track fun followed in Venezuela (September) and Mexico (October), as *Queen's Greatest Hits* started its

**Freddie at Live Aid.**

three-year album chart residency back in Britain. Kicking off with the inevitable 'Bohemian Rhapsody' and signing off with 'We Are The Champions', it was a solid gold, 17-track treat that found its way into many a Christmas stocking around the world.

Even better was to come. Six years after 'Bohemian Rhapsody', Queen clocked up their second UK Number 1 single, 'Under Pressure', recorded with a little help from guest vocalist David Bowie and rated by Roger Taylor as "one of the very best things we have ever done."

The Bowie link happened because he lived near the studio and sometimes popped over for a neighbourly drink. "Someone suggested that we should all go into the studio and play around one night to see what came out," explained Brian. "The next night, we listened to the tapes, picked out a couple of pieces and worked on one particular idea." That became 'Under Pressure' which, apart from its UK success, reached the US Number 29 slot.

**At full speed, Freddie in Wembley, 1986.**

An adoring crowd anxiously await the arrival of their heroes in the heat at Wembley.

> **"The next night, we listened to the tapes, picked out a couple of pieces and worked on one particular idea."**
> *Brian May*

### Rhythm rules

Roger Taylor took his own step toward a solo career earlier in the year with his first LP, *Fun In Space*. Released in April, it included the single 'Future Management' and its highest UK chart position was Number 18.

The first three months of 1982 were spent in Mountain Studios, Montreux, Switzerland, a complex Queen were to make their own in the coming years. *Hot Space* was the result, a funky album which reached Number 4 in Britain.

Again, rhythm ruled the roost, with tracks like 'Dancer' evolving from a backing track of

**Performing for the cameras at Live Aid.**

### Topless in Budapest.

bass and drums. Another song, 'Backchat', nearly didn't have a guitar solo at all—heresy to long-time Queen fans—because writer John Deacon wanted to produce an uncompromising R&B track. However, Brian edged his way in with an aggressive guitar sound to complement the backing perfectly.

Once out of the studio, a concert at Milton Keynes Bowl in June was recorded for British television's Channel 4 and broadcast as the band jetted off for three months' tour of the States and Japan.

While in America, Freddie bought an apartment in New York City. Nearby Boston was so grateful he'd become an honorary American that it declared a "Queen Day". Simultaneously, the *Guinness Book Of Records* listed the band as the world's highest paid executives.

### Going solo

It's a typical big-band story, but after 12 years at the very top of rock, it was a time for a break; they "were getting on each others' nerves,"

**A happy Deacon at an Eighties soundcheck.**

admitted Brian. The guitarist marked 1983 with the solo *Star Fleet Project*, which he shared with heavy metal superstar Eddie Van Halen, both men clearly unafraid of comparisons.

Since Freddie didn't want to re-sign with their American label, Elektra, Queen moved to Capitol Records. And as John surfed and Roger skied, Freddie re-entered the studio in Munich to start work on his first solo album, although it would be some time before this saw the light of day.

The solo work and long holidays were not an indication of a split, and by 1984 Queen were back together in (apparently) rejuvenated form, working on album number 13. Recorded in Germany with co-producer Mack, *The Works* wasn't unlucky, topping the charts in 19 countries (though only reaching the UK Number 2). It was a real team effort, full of what Brian called Queen's "over-the-top harmonies."

Much later, however, Brian revealed that the break from each other hadn't helped and that this was the worst period ever for relations within the band. "We did hate each other for a while. Recording *The Works*, we got very angry with each other. I left the group a couple of times—just for the day, you know. 'I'm off and I'm not coming back!' We've all done that. You end up quibbling over one note."

## Radio Ga Ga

The track most people will remember this album for is 'Radio Ga Ga', the UK Number 2 hit single

**Extreme close-up! Freddie caught on film.**

> **"We did hate each other for a while. Recording *The Works*, we got very angry with each other. I left the group a couple of times – just for the day, you know. I'm off and I'm not coming back! We've all done that. You end up quibbling over one note."**
> ***Brian May***

written by Roger. "There are some very difficult chords," he admitted later. "I don't know what they're called, but it doesn't matter as Spike [Edney, Queen's on-stage keyboardist] knows."

'Radio Ga Ga' owed its contemporary sound to a chart dominated by Soft Cell and Depeche Mode through having been composed on keyboard, but a second single from the LP, 'I Want To Break Free', was typically Queen. It reached Number 3 in Britain with the help of an outrageous Freddie fantasy video based on the British

**Freddie contemplates in a quiet moment.**

**Few groups have the pull to fill Wembley.**

TV soap opera *Coronation Street*, and featured the band in drag.

In May, Queen lip-synched to 400 million viewers at TV's *Golden Rose of Montreux* festival, as Roger Taylor's second solo album, *Strange Frontier*, climbed the UK charts to reach Number 30 in June. It included two cover versions of songs from classic writers he admired: Bruce Springsteen ('Racing In The Street') and Bob Dylan ('Masters Of War'), but as ever, Roger's own ideas found less acceptance than group releases.

In July, the band put in extensive rehearsals, some lasting more than 12 hours a day, to knock the rust off their performances and put them in shape to tour from August to November.

There was also a new film soundtrack for Fritz Lang's classic silent science fiction film *Metropolis* (from which Freddie had borrowed footage for the 'Radio Ga-Ga' video). It was released in October and included Freddie's first solo track, 'Love Kills' (also a Top 10 single), while 'Thank God It's Christmas' was the band's first seasonal single and staying in the chart all December.

## Disposable camp and cross-dressing

Given the effect Queen's music had on millions of fans, Freddie had a neat line in putting himself down. "I don't want to change the world with our music," was his astonishing claim. "There are no hidden messages in our songs,

**Hamming it up for the 'Radio Ga Ga' video.**

**Poetry in motion as Freddie goes solo.**

except for some of Brian's. I like to write songs for modern consumption. People can discard them like a used tissue afterwards. You listen to it, like it, discard it, then on to the next."

In fashion terms, the rest of the world had finally caught up with Freddie Mercury. "When I started off, rock bands were all wearing jeans, and suddenly here's Freddie Mercury in a Zandra Rhodes frock with make-up and black nail varnish. It was totally outrageous. In a way, Boy George has just updated that... it's the same outrage, just doubled."

Freddie's combination of on-stage extroversion and off-stage privacy found a soul mate in Michael Jackson. The duo cut a number of tracks

A very candid moment from one of Freddie's solo singles.

at Jackson's home studio, which unfortunately remained unreleased. And after Jackson's mega-successful album *Thriller*, the two drifted apart in a sad prediction of Freddie's own future. "He's simply retreated into a world of his own," he sighed in 1984.

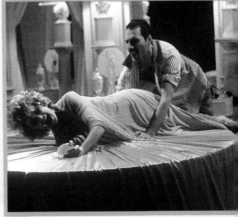

**A romantic interlude.**

**Power! John and Brian letting rip on stage.**

Freddie partied on regardless. His bashes frequently lasted weeks, and footage from one was used as a bonus for fans on one of his promo videos. One American junket staged for his 35th birthday, scheduled to run three days, ended up lasting a month. The bills included £50,000-plus ($75,000) for champagne, return Concorde tickets and a Cartier watch for each guest!

## Forced from the closet

To many fans (and those less well disposed toward him), Freddie's fishnet tights-style of on-stage camp was just another typical pop gimmick; his trademark. But to London's gay community, well into its dance music stride, Freddie represented something else. They knew. And then in February 1984, Freddie broke his dignified silence about his private life to protest at a tabloid story headlined, "Oh yes, I'm gay. I've done all that."

Freddie's furious response, admittedly seasoned with the odd deleted expletive, was: "For God's sake, if I wanted to make big confessions about my sex life, would I go to *The Sun* [Britain's top-selling tabloid daily newspaper], of all papers, to do it? There's no way I'd do that. I'm too intelligent."

Unlike Elton John, Freddie didn't have to undergo the hassle of a trial by tabloid, but his desire for privacy would become more marked as the decade went on. And that would inevitably have repercussions for Queen's future as a performing band.

**Cloaked in concert.**

# Live Aid and after

**Q**ueen kicked off 1985 with two shows at the mighty Rock In Rio festival in January, while a Far East tour took up April and May. But July was marked by the biggest rock concert the world had ever seen—Live Aid—and Queen, naturally, were the hit of the day. The fact they appeared at all was tribute to Bob Geldof's powers of persistence and persuasion. The Boomtown Rats' frontman had to chase Queen's manager, Jim Beach, halfway around the world, from England to New Zealand, to get the all-clear for Queen to appear.

Live Aid was to be the biggest rock spectacle ever, and Freddie revelled in it. "I'm so powerful on-stage that I seem to have created a monster. When I'm performing I'm an extrovert, yet inside I'm a completely different man."

Queen turned in a stunning set that showcased 'Radio Ga Ga' and 'Hammer To Fall'. "We don't do enough shows these days, and I'd like to do more," said an exhilarated Brian. 'I'll remember Live Aid till the day I die." It even

**One of the more surreal videos.**

brought a glowing tribute from the normally unquotable John Deacon: "It was the one day I was proud to be in the music business," said Queen's quiet man.

## Sadness, torture, pain

Freddie's long-playing solo debut, *Mr Bad Guy*, appeared in May and reached Number 6 in the UK chart. The Mercury muse apparently struck at the most inconvenient moments. "I actually dragged an upright piano to my bedside once," he claimed, adding implausibly, "I've been known to scribble lyrics in the middle of the night without putting the lights on."

He may have written in the dark, but it was clear he was poking fun at the image he'd created. Titles like 'Let's Turn It On', 'Foolin' Around' and 'My Love Is Dangerous' told one side of the story—but musically there was a lot more than humour on offer, if you looked beneath the surface.

"Many of the songs were relationship-centred," he admitted. "Most of my songs are love

**Freddie—triumphant!**

ballads and things to do with sadness and torture and pain. I seem to write a lot of sad songs because I'm a very tragic person." Outwardly, Freddie had plenty of friends. And no wonder: "Darling, I'm simply dripping with money," he once admitted. "It may be vulgar but it's wonderful! All I want from life is to make lots of money and spend it."

Behind the public extrovert, however, lived a very private man whose difficulty in establishing long-term relationships was clearly a source of immense private sorrow. The band, despite its ups and downs, remained the surrogate family, and he denied any plans to leave. "I've wanted to do a solo album for a long time," he explained, "and the rest of the band have encouraged me to do it."

Solo success didn't spell the end of Queen—far from it. "It's probably brought us closer together and will enhance our careers. It's like painting a picture. You have to step away from it to see what it's like. I'm stepping away from Queen and I think it's going to give everybody a shot in the arm. But I'll be working with Queen again. No doubt about that. Queen are gonna come back even bigger."

## Friends will be friends

He was right. By coincidence or design, the next Queen single—the Live Aid-inspired 'One Vision'

**Roger Taylor during the Knebworth concert.**

> **"Darling, I'm simply dripping with money, it may be vulgar but it's wonderful! All I want from life is to make lots of money and spend it."**
> *Freddie Mercury*

in November—released exactly ten years after 'Bohemian Rhapsody', went to Number 7 in the UK charts. And December proved to be an expensive month for collectors. All the Queen albums were released in a box-set—*Complete Works*—with an additional album of rarities called *Complete Vision*.

After a quiet start, 1986 heralded a flurry of action: in May, Queen's 'A Kind Of Magic' shot to UK Number 1; John's first solo single, 'No Turning Back', failed to chart at all; meanwhile, Freddie's rendition of the title theme of the Dave Clark stage musical *Time* reached Number

**Brian in cuddle mode with Anita Dobson.**

**Fluorescent's the thing at Knebworth.**

24. 'A Kind Of Magic' was written for the Russell Mulcahy film *Highlander*, its title being a line of actor Christopher Lambert's dialogue that Roger Taylor used. Brian May was being quiet, but possibly because his name was being romantically linked with actress Anita Dobson—Angie Watts in British TV soap opera *EastEnders*.

In June came 'Friends Will Be Friends', which

reached UK Number 14, followed less auspiciously by the *Biggles* film soundtrack, credited to John Deacon and The Immortals. With titles like 'Do You Want To Be A Hero', 'Chocks Away' and 'Aerial Pursuit', it was only for fanatic collectors (or possibly aeronauts).

Like its title track, the Queen album for 1986, *A Kind Of Magic*, featured music from the film *Highlander*. It went Number 1 in the UK LP chart, where it stayed for 13 straight weeks, playing a big part in Queen's total of 1.8 million albums sold that year. 'One Vision' featured, while 'Friends Will Be Friends'—a rare Mercury/Deacon collaboration—was a specially strong third single.

### The great pretender

The European Magic tour played to over a million, including Hungary—still behind the Iron Curtain in those days, where 80,000 people packed Budapest's Nep Stadium. Freddie's version of a Hungarian folk song, 'Tavaski Szel', brought the house down.

After selling out Wembley, the outdoor Knebworth one-day show in August, with a crowd of 120,000, was to prove the last ever UK Queen concert.

Fans could relive the experience in December with the release of *Live Magic*, which, even without a single release, sold 400,000 copies by

**Meeting his vocal match, Montserrat Caballé.**

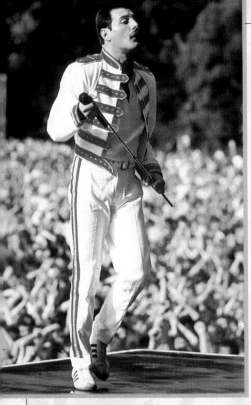

**Limbering up for action at Knebworth.**

> **"I just think she has this remarkable voice. I happened to mention it and she called me up."**
> *Freddie Mercury*

Christmas and reached UK Number 3.

During 1987, the band took most of the year off from touring and got away from each other again. In March 'The Great Pretender' became Freddie's highest charting solo single to date, which he celebrated with one of his most outrageous video drag acts ever. The song was a showcase for his powerful voice, but as if to prove to any critics that he was nothing but a pop singer, he topped even this in October with a new collaborator, a queen in her chosen field—Spanish opera singer Montserrat Caballé.

Their single, 'Barcelona', stayed in the British Top 10 for several weeks, probably because its power transcended its novelty effect, possibly

**Roger Taylor goes solo with his *Fun in Space* album and tour.**

because the novelty was itself enough. The unlikely collaboration came about by accident, claimed Freddie, because of a chance remark on Spanish television: "I just think she has this remarkable voice. I happened to mention it and she called me up."

### Getting cross

Not to be outdone, in July Roger Taylor auditioned members for his new group, Cross. He was to be the group's lead singer and rhythm guitarist, with Queen stage keyboardist Spike Edney also on the team.

Cross released their first album, *Shove It* (one track, 'Heaven For Everyone', featured Freddie on vocals), in January 1988. It spent only two weeks in the UK chart, peaking at Number 58. "We intend to build a powerbase with the intensity of our live performance," insisted an undaunted Taylor. "I think it'll be a force to be reckoned within six months." Brian and John joined Cross on-stage at London's Hammersmith

**Queen, ready to fly above millions of fans.**

Palais, reforming three-quarters of Queen for the night, with Freddie conspicuous by his absence.

'Bohemian Rhapsody' reappeared in September 1987—not the classic version but a parody by the *Young Ones* characters from the zany British television comedy programme and their spin-off group Bad News. Displaying his sense of humour, Brian May produced the record—and the group responded with a specially written B-side, 'Life With Brian'.

"I think we made a great record," said the

proud producer of the largely unscripted live performance, "but unfortunately it's not the kind of thing that can get commercial success as it's directed at a minority audience." He wasn't quite right because it charted, proving he was right to refer to it as "a very astute comment on rock music and the way that it's moved over the last few years."

It wasn't his only stint as producer. Many considered both his choices at the time as "odd"; the first was in June when he produced his actress girlfriend Anita Dobson's album, *Talking Of Love*. "Most of Anita's audience may have thought that it was getting too heavy," he admitted, "and most of those in my world thought, 'What the hell's he doing with someone who's really only a show-tune singer?' I stand by the project as being very worthwhile."

### I want to be alone

Around this time, Freddie decided he'd had enough of being at the centre of press attention and retreated to his 28-room Kensington mansion, with its 10-foot walls to keep the world at bay. "I want my privacy," he confirmed, "and I

**"I think I'm a bit old for leotards now."**

> **"We intend to build a powerbase with the intensity of our live performance, I think it'll be a force to be reckoned within six months."**
> *Roger Taylor*

feel I've given a lot for it. It's like Greta Garbo isn't it? Virgo, same star sign."

If his appetite for the limelight had decreased dramatically, his personal priorities, he revealed in a rare interview that again hinted strongly at his gay lifestyle, had changed just as dramatically: "I lived for sex. Amazingly, I've just gone completely the other way. AIDS changed my life. I have stopped going out, I've become almost a nun. I was extremely promiscuous, but I've stopped all that. What's more, I don't miss that kind of life."

As though to emphasise his withdrawal from

**The Cross—five lean hombres looking mean.**

**Sophisticated types, Roger and Brian, in company with Anita Dobson and friend, attending one of many awards functions.**

the hurly-burly of rock, in October he teamed up again with Montserrat Caballé to launch a joint-album (described by the record company as "a

glorious celebration of the power of pop and the passion of opera"). They started first in Barcelona itself, where ballet star Rudolf Nureyev was among the supporting cast, then at the Royal Opera House in London. The work received a mixed press reaction—some critics considered it a trivialization of opera and not even good pop—while the public pushed it to a UK Number 25.

Nevertheless, real Queen fans wanted Queen all together, on form and on-stage. They were to be disappointed.

## Too old for a leotard

Queen's forthcoming album, *The Miracle*, was previewed at the Queen Fan Convention in April 1989, but much of the thrill faded the moment Freddie announced he wouldn't tour in the fore-seeable future. "I've personally had it with these bombastic lights and staging effects," he stated in a written communiqué, adding with a chilling air of finality: "I don't think a 42-year-old man

*Live Magic* with Freddie Mercury in unstoppable form at Wembley in 1988.

<blockquote>
**"I've personally had it with these bombastic lights and staging effects, I don't think a 42-year-old man should be running around in his leotard any more."**
*Freddie Mercury*
</blockquote>

should be running around in his leotard any more."

It didn't yet signify the demise of Queen as a band. Freddie offered a crumb of comfort when he said, "I used to think we'd last five years, but it's got to the point where we're actually too old to break up. Can you imagine forming a new band at 40? Be a bit silly, wouldn't it?"

Absence had clearly made the public's heart grow fonder. 'I Want It All' reached the UK charts at Number 3 in May as a taster for *The Miracle*, which entered at Number 1 the following month. It was a real return to form. "I think

**Queen with some youthful stunt doubles together on set in the 'Scandal' video.**

a lot of people missed the typical Queen sound on our last few releases," was Roger Taylor's assessment of the new album. "*The Miracle* includes all of Queen's typical elements in concentrated form. If you listen carefully, you can hear all the built-in references to our past albums."

A Queen retrospective, then? Brian pinpointed other factors that, in a sense, confirmed the "look back" sound. "When we met to work on the new material, we only had drums, guitar, bass, vocals and keyboards—the classic line-up.

**Only their mothers can tell them apart.**

**Left: Smart suits and slicked-back hair for *Innuendo*'s photo session.**

That's how everything started. And that's basically how everything's stayed. Maybe that's the reason why *The Miracle* sounds more original and real. We left our egos outside the studio door and worked together as a real band."

"It was okay," was Freddie's less dramatic verdict on the recording sessions, "but we had our various fisticuffs."

## Beeb Beeb Queen

Two more Top 20 singles followed, in July ('Breakthru') and August ('The Invisible Man'), and *Rare Live* hit the video shops in the same month. It was a Queen collection video cassette, starting with the earliest footage (1973 in a rehearsal studio) and covering every stage of their career, including the first ever performances of many songs.

Brian made a rare stage appearance at a Jerry Lee Lewis concert at London's Hammersmith Odeon in December, just before *Queen At The Beeb*, an eight-track BBC radio compilation

**A wild rock look for a BBC session in 1973.**

"**Maybe that's the reason why *The Miracle* sounds more original and real. We left our egos outside the studio door and worked together as a real band.**"
***Brian May***

**A Taylor in the Seventies at the BBC session.**

from 1973, spent one week in the album chart as the group worked on ideas for their next album at Mountain Studios in Switzerland.

1990 started sensationally when the foursome appeared together—an event in itself—to pick up an award for their Outstanding Contribution to British Music at the Brit Awards in February. But there were comments about Freddie's state of health—he didn't look well. "It's true that he's been quite rough recently," admitted Brian when questioned. "I think his wild rock 'n' roll lifestyle has caught up with him. He just needs a break."

## Will Shakespeare work?

Roger Taylor's Cross released their second album, *Mad, Bad And Dangerous To Know*, in March, but it didn't chart. It's just as well Queen still played the dominant role in his musical ambitions. "You just have to subjugate egos and put the band first, before yourself, before your private life. Total faith and loyalty to the band is the thing that you need," he said stoutly.

Yet he also insisted that he needed to retain the challenge of playing live. "Queen is like a huge rolling machine, and we're not working all the time. I am a musician by profession, that's my whole life, and I didn't want to waste it in easy retirement."

Brian obviously shared this view for, missing the stage, he was out and about again in September, this time with Black Sabbath at Hammersmith. When not playing with others, he busied himself providing the music for a theatre production of *Macbeth*. Mixing Queen and the Bard was unlikely to appeal to everybody, and he was aware that "the music could be irritating if not done well," but he was also adamant that

**The all-smiling, angelic features of Brian.**

**Brian May and Adrian Edmondson from the spoof group Bad News.**

**Right: John Deacon at a BBC radio session.**

"Will Shakespeare was into making direct contact with his audience—a lot like Queen has always done."

When unknown US rapper Vanilla Ice shot to the top of the UK singles chart with 'Ice Ice Baby', a rap track incorporating the distinctive bass line from Queen's 'Under Pressure', the matter was settled out of court. "I just thought, interesting, but nobody will ever buy it because it's crap. Turns out I was wrong," commented a chastened Brian May.

## Hollywood pays

After a year's silence, 'Innuendo' entered the UK singles listings at Number 1 in January 1991—the first ever Queen single to do so and, at over 6 minutes, the longest UK Number 1 single since 'Bohemian Rhapsody'. The video, too, though a contemporary production from a group always ahead of the times, had echoes of 1975.

That Queen's popularity was still riding high was evidenced when *Greatest Hits* re-entered the UK album charts in February in the wake of

> **"Will Shakespeare was into making direct contact with his audience – a lot like Queen has always done."**
> *Brian May*

the single's success. But it was soon replaced by *Innuendo*, a UK Number 1 album and the first Queen album to appear (in America only) on Walt Disney's Hollywood Records, who paid a reported $10 million (£6.6 million) for the rights to Queen's US releases.

*Innuendo* had much in common with Seventies' Queen classics like *A Night At The Opera*, with many overdubs and much musical complexity. 'Headlong' and 'I Can't Live With You' were

**Queen in Geneva in 1988.**

Freddie in his element. All he needs is 'Radio Ga Ga'.

typically passionate, guitar-laden Brian May tracks; 'Headlong', indeed, was the third single to be taken from the album, preceded by Freddie's wacky 'I'm Going Slightly Mad' (on the video he did a Carmen Miranda and wore a bunch of bananas).

## The show must go on

As Queen returned to Montreux to record more new material, 'The Stonk'—the charity Comic Relief theme song sung by Hale and Pace and produced by Brian—reached Number 1 in the UK singles chart. But no new songs were to be recorded at Montreux. Rumours about Freddie's health were growing as the November release of their second hits compilation neared. Even the single that accompanied it, 'The Show Must Go On', suggested impending tragedy. Finally, on November 23, 1991, the worst was confirmed.

"Following the enormous conjecture in the

**Left: The remaining members of Queen shortly after Freddie's death.**
**Right: Happier days—a bizarre costume from the 'I'm Going Slightly Mad' video.**

Brian reveals he has always had a secret desire to be a penguin with frizzy hair.

> **"Following the enormous conjecture in the press over the last two weeks, I wish to confirm that I have been tested HIV-positive and have AIDS."**
> *Freddie Mercury*

press over the last two weeks," a statement read, "I wish to confirm that I have been tested HIV-positive and have AIDS.

"I felt it correct to keep this information private to date to protect the privacy of those around me. However, the time has come now for my friends and fans around the world to know the truth and I hope that everyone will join with my doctors and all those worldwide in the fight against this terrible disease.

"My privacy has always been very special to

me and I am famous for my lack of interviews. Please understand this policy will continue."

Freddie Mercury died the following day. He was showman to the last. It's bad enough for fans to discover that their idol has a terminal illness; to tell them the day before it takes its toll makes for extreme drama.

In one of his last interviews, he explained why he'd quietened down so much: "I can't carry on rocking the way I have done in the past. It's no way for a grown man to behave. I have stopped my nights of wild partying. That's not because I'm ill but down to age. I'm no spring chicken. Now I prefer to spend my time at home."

His death at the age of 45 on November 24, 1991, robbed rock music of a major talent. But his music will live on—something he recognized back in the Eighties. "If everything you read about me in the press was true, I would have burnt myself out by now. We will stick to our guns, and if worth anything we will live on."

**This is the sort of costume you get if you call a song 'I'm Going Slightly Mad'.**

George Michael joins the remaining members of Queen for a version of the song '39'.

# The legend lives on

Without their lead singer, Brian, Roger and John made it immediately clear that Queen could not continue. "As far as we are concerned," said Roger, "that is it. There's no point going on. It is impossible to replace Freddie. We feel overwhelming grief that he's gone, but great pride in the courageous way he lived and died. It has been a privilege to share such magical times."

Brian May added his own tribute in an interview on a British breakfast television programme: "We knew instinctively something was going on but it was not talked about. He did not officially tell us until a few months ago. Certainly he knew for five years or so. He was living under a shadow for a very long time.

"He made the crucial decision to disclose he had AIDS. It would have been very easy to put on his death certificate 'pneumonia', and it could have sidestepped everything. He said 'I've got this and there is no shame—no stigma'."

The press was kinder to Freddie Mercury in death than it had sometimes been to him during the band's glory years. Nevertheless, his funeral on November 27 was staked out by the usual posse of cameramen after a story, who were rewarded by Elton John as a rare star mourner among 35 family and close friends. "Thanks for being my friend," read Elton's card attached to a hundred pink roses. "I will love you always."

## An open mind

Verbal tributes came from far and wide. Phil Collins, David Bowie, Dave Clark, the Moody Blues' Justin Hayward and countless other stars recorded their admiration.

Perhaps the most moving tribute came from Axl Rose, lead singer of Guns N' Roses. Well

**Freddie clearly altered in one of the last photo shoots for *Innuendo*.**

**Freddie having a sing song with former topless model, vocalist Samantha Fox.**

known for his anti-gay views expressed in the objectionable lyric of 'One In A Million', he revealed that Queen had been a formative influence on his youth. "If I hadn't had Freddie Mercury's lyrics to hold on to as a kid," he said, "I don't know where I would be. It taught me about all forms of music... it would open my mind. I never really had a bigger teacher in my whole life."

Elsewhere, EMI (still Queen's record label after two decades) looked for a way to commemorate Freddie Mercury's passing. Six tracks had been recorded for but not included on *Innuendo*, and it was suggested these could quickly be made ready for posthumous release. Thankfully, a more fitting musical tribute was paid by the reissue of 'Bohemian Rhapsody', backed with the poignant 'These Are The Days Of Our Lives'. The AIDS charity, The Terrence Higgins Trust, benefited from the royalties when it became a Christmas Number 1, adding five more weeks to its time atop the UK singles chart. Curiously, its nine previous weeks at Number 1 had spanned another Christmas, 1975, giving it a place in the

> **"It is impossible to replace Freddie. We feel overwhelming grief that he's gone, but great pride in the courageous way he lived and died. It has been a privilege to share such magical times."**
> *Roger Taylor*

pop trivia books to add to its undoubted classic status.

## Champions again

On April 20, 1992, London's Wembley Stadium hosted a veritable galaxy of stars who came to pay tribute to Freddie Mercury's unique talent. Elton John, Guns N' Roses, Extreme, Metallica, Def Leppard, even Liza Minnelli—all these and more gathered "to give Freddie a proper send-off," as Brian May put it. All 72,000 tickets sold out in six hours, with a fervour that put even Live Aid in the shade. Roger Taylor saw the event as "a memorial service. It's a way of saying goodbye to Freddie."

**Freddie in his prime around 1974.**

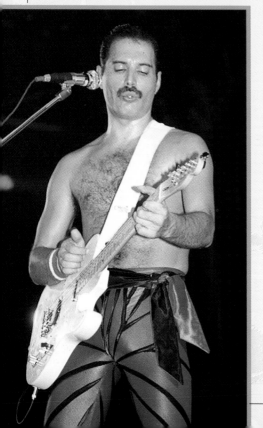

> **"If I hadn't had Freddie Mercury's lyrics to hold on to as a kid, I don't know where I would be. It taught me about all forms of music."**
> *Axl Rose*

The day's highlights were many and varied: Mick Ronson, Ian Hunter and David Bowie singing 'All The Young Dudes' (tragically, within 18 months Ronson would be dead through cancer); George Michael offering 'Days Of Our Lives' with Lisa Stansfield and 'Somebody To Love' (later extracted as a chart-topping live single to benefit charity); The Who's Roger Daltrey giving his all on 'I Want It All'; and Def Leppard singer Joe Elliott duelling with Guns N' Roses guitarist Slash on 'Tie Your Mother Down'.

The finale, led by Liza Minnelli, was

**Joining in on guitar at the Budapest concert in 1986.**

inevitable: 'We Are The Champions', with scarcely a dry eye on-stage or in the audience. Having just been bludgeoned into submission by Axl Rose's 'We Will Rock You' (he'd earlier duetted sensationally with Elton John on 'Bohemian Rhapsody'), the crowd were content to say goodbye with a massed burst of community singing.

As Brian May said in introducing Minnelli, Freddie would have been thrilled to see one of his favourite performers singing his own song. That he couldn't be there in person was the only regret of a joyous day.

### Repackaged

But there were other joys to come. Brian May had played a poignant new song at Wembley, 'Too Much Love Will Kill You', which became a Top 5 hit in late 1992, while a double-album of music from the band's last tour was issued as *Live At Wembley 1986*, reminding fans once again of the showman they had lost.

Most surprising of all, however, was a remixed, remodelled and highly contemporary dance version of 'Living On My Own'. A club hit

**Friends and relatives attending Freddie Mercury's funeral 1991.**

when issued as a limited vinyl pressing by mix-masters Colin Peter and Carl Ward (The Brothers Organisation) and producer Serge Ramaekers, it

**The thousands of wreaths given by fans.**

was accorded a wider airing by public demand in July 1993, and ended up a UK summer Number 1.

The song had been very special to Freddie himself, as he'd revealed at the time of its original release on *Mr Bad Guy*: "'Living On My Own' is very me. I have to go around the world living in hotels. You can have a whole shoal of people you know looking after you, but in the end they all go away."

The original mix (it had peaked at Number 50 when first issued in 1985) popped up again on The *Freddie Mercury Album*, a coldly calculated repackaging of material from *Mr Bad Guy* and *Barcelona* that appeared in November 1992 and charted in the UK at Number 4 in the Christmas rush.

## Aftermath

Roger Taylor finally disbanded Cross in 1993, having earlier guested with veteran rocker Shakin' Stevens on a single, 'Radio', which just scraped into the UK Top 40. It seemed likely he'd take a break from the spotlight and pick up the threads of a production career that had already included work with such names as ex-Undertone Feargal Sharkey, singing actor Jimmy Nail and shock-rockers Sigue Sigue Sputnik.

Brian May, meanwhile, found a career in his own right as easy as falling off a wooden fireplace... yes, he was still playing his home-made guitar! He recorded a hit solo album, *Back To The Light*, toured Britain successfully and reached the UK Number 6 slot with the single 'Driven By You'—the Ford television commercial theme—in late 1991. In the following year he joined boyhood idol Hank Marvin of the Shadows for a twangy instrumental version of 'We Are The Champions'. Of John Deacon, little was heard.

Rumours persist of previously unreleased Mercury-era material to come. Rumours persist about what the surviving members of Queen will

**Queen parties attracted stars like Sigue Sigue Sputnik and Janet Street-Porter.**

do as artists and producers. Yet even if, like Deacon, they choose to escape from the public eye, they have already done enough to secure their place in rock's all-time hall of fame.

Queen live on in the showmanship of Axl Rose, the energy of Extreme, the multi-layered harmonies of Def Leppard. All these acts, and more, ensure that the legacy of Freddie Mercury and his merry men will reverberate anew for future generations to enjoy.

# COMPLETE QUEEN & SOLO DISCOGRAPHY

## PRE-QUEEN SINGLES

### SMILE
Earth/Step On Me
Mercury 72977. US release only.

### SMILE EP
Doing Alright/Blag/April Lady/Polar
Bear/Earth/Step On Me
Japanese release only.

### LARRY LUREX
I Can Hear Music/Goin' Back
EMI 2030. Release date June 1973.
Highest UK chart position: Number -.

## QUEEN SINGLES

Keep Yourself Alive/Son And Daughter
EMI 2036. Release date July 1973.
Highest UK chart position: Number -.

Seven Seas Of Rhye/See What A Fool I've
Been
EMI 2121. Release date February 1974.
Highest UK chart position: Number 10.

Killer Queen/Flick Of The Wrist
EMI 2229. Release date October 1974.
Highest UK chart position: Number 2.

Now I'm Here/Lily Of The Valley
EMI 2256. Release date January 1975.
Highest UK chart position: Number 11.

Bohemian Rhapsody/I'm In Love With My
Car
EMI 2375. Release date October 1975.
Highest UK chart position: Number 1.

You're My Best Friend/'39
EMI 2494. Release date July 1976.
Highest UK chart position: Number 7.

Somebody To Love/White Man
EMI 2565. Release date November 1976.
Highest UK chart position: Number 2.

Tie Your Mother Down/You And I
EMI 2593. Release date March 1977.
Highest UK chart position: Number 31.

### Queen EP

Good Old Fashioned Loverboy/Death On
Two Legs/Tenement Funster/White
Queen
EMI 2623. Release date June 1977.
Highest UK chart position: Number 17.

We Are The Champions/We Will Rock
You
EMI 2708. Release date October 1977.
Highest UK chart position: Number 2.

Spread Your Wings/
Sheer Heart Attack
EMI 2757. Release date February 1978.
Highest UK chart position: Number 34.

Bicycle Race/Fat Bottomed Girls
(Double A-side)
EMI 2870. Release date October 1978.
Highest UK chart position: Number 11.

Don't Stop Me Now/In Only 7 Days
EMI 2910. Release date January 1979.
Highest UK chart position: Number 9.

Love Of My Life (Live)/Now I'm Here (Live)
EMI 2959. Release date June 1979.
Highest UK chart position: Number 63.

Crazy Little Thing Called Love/Spread
Your Wings (Live)
EMI 5001. Release date October 1979.
Highest UK chart position: Number 2.

Save Me/Let Me Entertain You (Live)
EMI 5022. Release date January 1980.
Highest UK chart position: Number 11.

Play The Game/A Human Body
EMI 5076. Release date May 1980.
Highest UK chart position: Number 14.

Another One Bites The Dust/Dragon
Attack
EMI 5102. Release date August 1980.
Highest UK chart position: Number 7.

Flash/Football Fight
EMI 5126. Release date November 1980.
Highest UK chart position: Number 10.

Under Pressure (with David Bowie)/Soul
Brother
EMI 5250. Release date November 1981.
Highest UK chart position: Number 1.

Body Language/Life Is Real
EMI 5293. Release date April 1982.
Highest UK chart position: Number 25.

Las Palabras De Amor/Cool Cat
EMI 5293. Release date June 1982.
Highest UK chart position: Number 17.

Backchat/Staying Power
EMI 4325. Release date August 1982.
Highest UK chart position: Number 40.

Radio Ga Ga/I Go Crazy
QUEEN 1. Release date January 1984.
Highest UK chart position: Number 2.

I Want To Break Free/Machines (Or Back
To Humans)
QUEEN 2. Release date April 1984.
Highest UK chart position: Number 3.

It's A Hard Life/Is This The World We
Created?
QUEEN 3. Release date July 1984.
Highest UK chart position: Number 6.

Hammer To Fall/Tear It Up
QUEEN 4. Release date September 1984.
Highest UK chart position: Number 13.

Thank God It's Christmas/Man On The Prowl/Keep Passing The Open Windows
QUEEN 5. Release date November 1984.
Highest UK chart position: Number 21.

One Vision/Blurred Vision
QUEEN 6. Release date November 1985.
Highest UK chart position: Number 7.

A Kind Of Magic/
A Dozen Red Roses For My Darling
QUEEN 7. Release date March 1986.
Highest UK chart position: Number 3.

Friends Will Be Friends/
Seven Seas Of Rhye
QUEEN 8. Release date June 1986.
Highest UK chart position: Number 14.

Who Wants To Live Forever?/
A Kind Of Magic/Killer Queen
QUEEN 9. Release date September 1986.
Highest UK chart position: Number 24.

I Want It All/Hang On In There
QUEEN 10. Release date May 1989.
Highest UK chart position: Number 3.

Breakthru/Stealin'
QUEEN 11. Release date June 1989.
Highest UK chart position: Number 7.

The Invisible Man/Hijack My Heart
QUEEN 12. Release date August 1989.
Highest UK chart position: Number 12.

Scandal/My Life Has Been Saved
QUEEN 14. Release date October 1989.
Highest UK chart position: Number 25.

The Miracle/Stone Cold Crazy (Live)
QUEEN 15. Release date November 1989.
Highest UK chart position: Number 21.

Innuendo/Bijou
QUEEN 16. Release date January 1991.
Highest UK chart position: Number 1.

I'm Going Slightly Mad/The Hitman
QUEEN 17. Release date March 1991.
Highest UK chart position: Number 22.

Headlong/All God's People
QUEEN 18. Release date May 1991.
Highest UK chart position: Number 14.

The Show Must Go On/
Keep Yourself Alive
QUEEN 19. Release date October 1991.
Highest UK chart position: Number 16.

Bohemian Rhapsody/
These Are The Days Of Our Lives
(Double A-side)
QUEEN 20. Release date December 1991.
Highest UK chart position: Number 1.

## ALBUMS

### QUEEN
EMI EMC 3006. Release date July 1973.
Highest UK chart position: Number 24.
Keep Yourself Alive
Doing All Right
Great King Rat
My Fairy King
Liar
The Night Comes Down
Modern Times Rock'n'roll

Son And Daughter
Jesus
Seven Seas Of Rhye

### QUEEN II
EMI EMA 767. Release date March 1974.
Highest UK chart position: Number 5.
Procession
Father To Son
White Queen (As It Began)
Some Day One Day
The Loser
Ogre Battle
The Fairy Fellow's Master Stroke
Nevermore
March Of The Black Queen
Funny How Love Is
Seven Seas Of Rhye

### SHEER HEART ATTACK
EMI EMC 3061. Release date November 1974.
Highest UK chart position: Number 2.
Brighton Rock
Killer Queen
Tenement Funster
Flick Of The Wrist
Lily Of The Valley
Now I'm Here
In The Lap Of The Gods
Stone Cold Crazy
Dear Friends
Misfire
Bring Back That Leroy Brown
She Makes Me (Stormtrooper In Stilettoes)
In The Lap Of The Gods... Revisited

### A NIGHT AT THE OPERA
EMI EMTC 103. Release date December 1975.
Highest UK chart position: Number 1.
Death On Two Legs (Dedicated To)
Lazing On A Sunday Afternoon
I'm In Love With My Car
You're My Best Friend
'39
Sweet Lady
Seaside Rendezvous
The Prophet's Song
Love Of My Life
Good Company
Bohemian Rhapsody
God Save The Queen

### A DAY AT THE RACES
EMI EMTC 104. Release date December 1976.
Highest UK chart position: Number 1.
Tie Your Mother Down
You Take My Breath Away
Long Away
The Millionaire Waltz
You And I
Somebody To Love
White Man
Good Old Fashioned Lover Boy
Drowse
Teo Torriate (Let Us Cling Together)

### NEWS OF THE WORLD
EMI EMA 784. Release date October 1977.
Highest UK chart position: Number 4.
We Will Rock You
We Are The Champions
Sheer Heart Attack
All Dead All Dead
Spread Your Wings
Fight From The Inside

Get Down Make Love
Sleeping On The Sidewalk
Who Needs You
It's Late
My Melancholy Blues

## JAZZ
EMI EMA 788. Release date November 1978.
Highest UK chart position: Number 2.
Mustapha
Fat Bottomed Girls
Jealousy
Bicycle Race
If You Can't Beat Them
Let Me Entertain You
Dead On Time
In Only Seven Days
Dreamer's Ball
Fun It
Leaving Home Ain't Easy
Don't Stop Me Now
More Of That Jazz

## LIVE KILLERS
EMI EMSP 330. Release date June 1979.
Highest UK chart position: Number 3.
We Will Rock You
Let Me Entertain You
Death On Two Legs
Killer Queen
Bicycle Race
I'm In Love With My Car
Get Down Make Love
You're My Best Friend
Now I'm Here
Dreamer's Ball
Love Of My Life

'39
Keep Yourself Alive
Don't Stop Me Now
Spread Your Wings
Brighton Rock
Mustapha
Bohemian Rhapsody
Tie Your Mother Down
Sheer Heart Attack
We Will Rock You
We Are The Champions
God Save The Queen

## THE GAME
EMI EMA 795. Release date June 1980.
Highest UK chart position: Number 1.
Play The Game
Dragon Attack
Another One Bites The Dust
Need Your Loving Tonight
Crazy Little Thing Called Love
Rock It (Prime Jive)
Don't Try Suicide
Sail Away Sweet Sister
Coming Soon
Save Me

## FLASH GORDON
EMI EMC 3351. Release date December 1980.
Highest UK chart position: Number 10.
Flash's Theme
In The Space Capsule (The Love Theme)
Ming's Theme (In The Court Of Ming The Merciless)
The Ring (Hypnotic Seduction Of Dale)
Football Fight
In The Death Cell (Love Theme Reprise)
Execution Of Flash

The Kiss (Aura Resurrects Flash)
Arboria (Planet Of The Tree Men)
Escape From The Swamp
Flash To The Rescue
Vultan's Theme (Attack Of The Hawk Men)
Battle Theme
The Wedding March
Marriage Of Dale And Ming (And Flash Approaching)
Crash Dive On Mingo City
Flash's Theme Reprise (Victory Celebrations)
The Hero

## GREATEST HITS
EMI EMTV 30. Release date October 1981.
Highest UK chart position: Number 1.
Bohemian Rhapsody
Another One Bites The Dust
Killer Queen
Fat Bottomed Girls
Bicycle Race
You're My Best Friend
Don't Stop Me Now
Save Me
Crazy Little Thing Called Love
Somebody To Love
Now I'm Here
Good Old Fashioned Lover Boy
Play The Game
Flash
Seven Seas Of Rhye
We Will Rock You
We Are The Champions

## HOT SPACE
EMI EMA 797. Release date May 1982.
Highest UK chart position: Number 4.

Staying Power
Dancer
Back Chat
Body Language
Action This Day
Put Out The Fire
Life Is Real (Song For Lennon)
Calling All Girls
Las Palabras De Amour (The Words Of Love)
Cool Cat
Under Pressure (with David Bowie)

## THE WORKS
EMI EMC 2400141. Release date February 1984.
Highest UK chart position: Number 2.
Radio Ga Ga
Tear It Up
It's A Hard Life
Man On The Prowl
Machines (Or Back To Humans)
I Want To Break Free
Keep Passing The Open Windows
Hammer To Fall
Is This The World We Created?

## THE COMPLETE WORKS
EMI QB1. Release date December 1985.
Highest UK chart position: Number -.
A boxed set of Queen's 11 studio and Live Killers albums, plus a new album compiling previously unaccounted for singles and B-sides:
See What A Fool I've Been
A Human Body
Soul Brother
I Go Crazy
Thank God It's Christmas

One Vision
Blurred Vision

A KIND OF MAGIC
EMI EU 3509. Release date May 1986.
Highest UK chart position: Number 1.
One Vision
A Kind Of Magic
One Year Of Love
Pain Is So Close To Pleasure
Friends Will Be Friends
Who Wants To Live Forever?
Gimme The Prize (Kurgan's Theme)
Don't Lose Your Head
Princes Of The Universe

LIVE MAGIC
EMI EMC 3509. Release date December 1986.
Highest UK chart position: Number 3.
One Vision
Tie Your Mother Down
Seven Seas Of Rhye
Another One Bites The Dust
I Want To Break Free
Is This The World We Created?
Bohemian Rhapsody
Hammer To Fall
Radio Ga Ga
We Will Rock You
Friends Will Be Friends
We Are The Champions
God Save The Queen
A Kind Of Magic
Under Pressure

QUEEN AT THE BEEB
Band Of Joy BOJ 001. Release date December 1989.

Highest UK chart position: Number 67.
My Fairy King
Keep Yourself Alive
Doing Alright
Liar
Ogre Battle
Great King Rat
Modern Times Rock'n'roll
Son And Daughter

THE MIRACLE
Parlophone PCSD 107. Release date May 1989.
Highest UK chart position: Number 1.
Party
Kashoggi's Ship
The Miracle
I Want It All
The Invisible Man
Breakthru
Rain Must Fall
Scandal
My Baby Does Me
Was It All Worth It
Hang on In There (CD only)
Chinese Torture (CD only)

INNUENDO
Parlophone PCSD 115. Release date February 1991.
Highest UK chart position: Number 1.
Innuendo
I'm Going Slightly Mad
Headlong
I Can't Like With You
Ride The Wild Wind
All God's People
These Are The Days Of Our Lives
Delilah

Don't Try So Hard
The Hitman
Bijou
The Show Must Go On

GREATEST HITS II
Parlophone PMTV 2. Release date November 1991.
Highest UK chart position: Number 1.
A Kind Of Magic
Under Pressure
I Want It All
I Want To Break Free
Innuendo
Breakthru
Who Wants To Live Forever?
Headlong
The Miracle
I'm Going Slightly Mad
The Invisible Man
Hammer To Fall
Friends Will Be Friends
The Show Must Go On

LIVE AT WEMBLEY '86
Parlophone CDPCSP 7251. Release date June 1992.
Highest UK chart position: Number 2.
One Vision
Tie Your Mother Down
In The Lap Of The Gods
Seven Seas Of Rhye
Tear It Up
A Kind Of Magic
Under Pressure
Another One Bites The Dust
Who Wants To Live Forever?
I Want To Break Free
Impromptu

Brighton Rock Solo
Now I'm Here
Love Of My Life
Is This The World We Created?
(You're So Square) Baby I Don't Care
Hello Mary Lou (Goodbye Heart)
Tutti Frutti
Gimme Some Lovin'
Bohemian Rhapsody
Hammer To Fall
Crazy Little Thing Called Love
Big Spender
Radio Ga Ga
We Will Rock You
Friends Will Be Friends
We Are The Champions
God Save The Queen

**FREDDIE MERCURY
SOLO SINGLES**

Love Kills/Rot Wang's Party
CBS A 4735. Release date September 1984.
Highest UK chart position: Number 10.

I Was Born To Love You/Stop All The Fighting
CBS A 6019. Release date May 1985.
Highest UK chart position: Number 11.

Made In Heaven/She Blows Hot And Cold
CBS A 6413. Release date July 1985.
Highest UK chart position: Number 57.

Living On My Own/My Love Is Dangerous
CBS A 6555. Release date September 1985.
Highest UK chart position: Number 50.

Love Me Like There's No Tomorrow/Let's Turn It On
CBS A 6725. Release date November 1985.
Highest UK chart position: Number -.

Time/Time (Instrumental)
EMI 5559. Release date May 1986.
Highest UK chart position: Number 32.

The Great Pretender/Exercises In Free Love
Parlophone R 6151. Release date March 1987.
Highest UK chart position: Number 4.

Barcelona/Exercises In Free Love (with Montserrat Caballé)
Polydor PO 887. Release date October 1987.
Highest UK chart position: Number 8.

The Golden Boy/The Fallen Priest (w/Caballé)
Polydor PO 23. Release date October 1988.
Highest UK chart position: Number -.

How Can I Go On/Overture Piccante (w/Caballé)
Polydor PO 29. Release date January 1989.
Highest UK chart position: Number 95.

In My Defence/Love Kills
EMI R 6331. Release date October 1992.
Highest UK chart position: Number 8.

The Great Pretender/Stop All The

Fighting
EMI R 6336. Release date January 1993.
Highest UK chart position: Number 29.

Living On My Own/Living On My Own (Mixes)
EMI R 6355. Release date July 1993.
Highest UK chart position: Number 1.

## FREDDIE MERCURY SOLO ALBUMS

### MR BAD GUY
CBS 86312. Release date May 1985.
Highest UK chart position: Number 6.
Let's Turn It On
Made In Heaven
I Was Born To Love You
Foolin' Around
Your Kind Of Lover
Mr Bad Guy
Man-Made Paradise
There Must Be More To Life Than This
Living On My Own
My Love Is Dangerous
Love Me Like There's No Tomorrow

### BARCELONA
(with Montserrat Caballé)
Polydor POLH 44. Release date October 1988.
Highest UK chart position: Number 25.
Barcelona
The Fallen Priest
The Golden Boy
Guide Me Home
Overture Piccante
La Japonaise
Ensueno

Guide Me Home
How Can I Go On

### THE FREDDIE MERCURY ALBUM
Parlophone CDPCSD 124. Release date November 1992.
Highest UK chart position: Number 4.
The Great Pretender
Foolin' Around
Time
Your Kind Of Lover
Exercises In Free Love
In My Defence
Mr Bad Guy
Let's Turn It On
Living On My Own
Love Kills
Barcelona

## BRIAN MAY SOLO SINGLES

Star Fleet/Son Of Star Fleet (and friends)
EMI 5436. Release date November 1983.
Highest UK chart position: Number 65.

Driven By You/Just One Life
Parlophone R 6304. Release date November 1991.
Highest UK chart position: Number 6.

Too Much Love Will Kill You/I'm Scared
Parlophone R 6320. Release date September 1992.
Highest UK chart position: Number 5.

We Are The Champions (with Hank Marvin)

PolyGram TV PO 229. Release date October 1992.
Highest UK chart position: Number 66.

Back To The Light/Nothin But Blue (guitar version)/Star Fleet
Parlophone R 6329. Release date November 1992.
Highest UK chart position: Number 19.

## BRIAN MAY SOLO ALBUMS

### STAR FLEET PROJECT
(with friends)
EMI SFLT 1078061. Release date
Highest UK chart position: Number 35.
Star Fleet
Let Me Out
Bluesbreaker

### BACK TO THE LIGHT
EMI PCSD 123. Release date October 1992.
Highest UK chart position: Number 6.
The Dark
Back To The Light
Love Token
Resurrection
Too Much Love Will Kill You
Driven By You
Nothin' But Blue
I'm Scared
Last Horizon
Let Your Heart Rule Your Head
Just One Life
Rollin' Over

**ROGER TAYLOR**
**SOLO SINGLES**

Future Management
EMI 5157. Release date April 1981.
Highest UK chart position: Number 49.

My Country/Step On The Gas
EMI 5200. Release date June 1981.
Highest UK chart position: Number -.

Man On Fire/Killing Time
EMI 5478. Release date June 1984.
Highest UK chart position: Number 66.

Strange Frontier/I Cry For You/Two Sharp
Pencils
EMI 5490. Release date August 1984.
Highest UK chart position: Number -.

Radio (with Shakin' Stevens)
Epic 6584367. Release date October 1992.
Highest UK chart position: Number 37.

**THE CROSS SINGLES**

Cowboys And Indians/Love Lies Bleeding
Virgin VS1007. Release date September
1987.
Highest UK chart position: Number 74.

Shove It/Rough Justice
Virgin VS1026. Release date January 1988.
Highest UK chart position: Number -.

Heaven For Everyone/Love On A
Tightrope (Like An Animal)
Virgin VS1062. Release date March 1988.
Highest UK chart position: Number -.

Shove It (Extended version)/Rough
Justice/Shove It (Metropolix)/Cowboys
And Indians
Virgin CDEP 20. Release date April 1988.
Highest UK chart position: Number -.

Manipulator/Stand Up For Love
Virgin VS1100. Release date July 1988.
Highest UK chart position: Number -.

Power To Love/Passion For Trash
Parlophone R6251. Release date April
1990
Highest UK chart position: Number -.

**SOLO ALBUMS**

**FUN IN SPACE**
EMI EMC 3369. Release date April 1981.
Highest UK chart position:
Number 18.
Fun In Space
No Violins
Laugh Or Cry
Let's Get Crazy
Future Management
My Country
Good Times Are Now
Magic Is Loose
Interlude In Constantinople
Airheads
**STRANGE FRONTIER**
EMI RTA 1. Release date June 1984.
Highest UK chart position: Number 30.
Strange Frontier
Beautiful Dreams
Man On Fire
Racing In The Street

Masters Of War
Killing Time
Abandonfire
Young Love
It's An Illusion
I Cry For You

**THE CROSS ALBUMS**

**SHOVE IT**
Virgin V2477. Release date November
1987.
Highest UK chart position: Number 58.
OVED302. Reissued April 1990.
Shove It
Heaven For Everyone
Love On A Tightrope (Like An Animal)
Cowboys And Indians
Stand Up For Love
Love Lies Bleeding (She Was A Wicked,
Wily Waitress)
Rough Justice
The 2nd Shelf Mix (CD only)
Contact

**MAD, BAD AND DANGEROUS
TO KNOW**
Parlophone PCS7342. Release date March
1990.
Highest UK chart position: Number -.
Top Of The World Ma
Liar
Closer To You
Break Down
Penetration Guru
Power To Love
Sister Blue
Foxy Lady (CD only)
Better Things

Passion For Trash
Old Men (Lay Down)
Final Destination

**JOHN DEACON and the
Immortals**

**SINGLE**

No Turning Back/No Turning Back (Chocs
Away Mix)
MCA 1057. Release date May 1986.
Highest UK chart position: Number -.

**ALBUM**

BIGGLES (Film Soundtrack LP)
MCA MCF 3328. Release date
June 1986.
Highest UK chart position: Number -.
Do You Want To Be A Hero
Chocks Away
Big Hot Blues
Knocking On Your Back Door
Knock 'Em Dead Kid
No Turning Back
Music Soundtrack
Ariel Pursuit
Discovery
Biggles Theme
Maria's Theme

# CHRONOLOGY

Freddie Mercury (Bulsara) born, September 5 1946
The Bulsara family moved to England, 1959
First Album *Queen* released, July 1973
Touring Britain, November-December 1973
Music Festival In Melbourne Australia, February 1974
*Queen II* released, March 1974
First U.K tour, March 1974
*Sheer Heart Attack* released, November 1974
'Bohemian Rapsody' released, October 1975
*A Night at the Opera* released, December 1975
*A Day at the Races* released, December 1976
*News of the World* released, October 1977
*Jazz* released, November 1978
*Live Killers* released, June 1979
*The Game* released, June 1980
*Flash Gordon* released, December 1980
First stadium tour of South America, February 1981
*Greatest Hits* released, October 1981
*Hot Space* released, May 1982
*The Works* released, February 1984
Rock in Rio Festival, January 1985
Far East tour, April-May 1985
Live Aid, July 1985
*The Complete Works* released, December 1985
American tour, February 1986
Japanese tour, March 1986
Australian tour, April 1986
*A Kind of Magic* released, May 1986

Free concert Hyde Park, London, September 1986
*Live Magic* released, December 1986
*The Miracle* previewed at the Queen fan convention, April 1989
*The Miracle* released, May 1989
*Queen at the Beeb* released, December 1989
*Innuendo* released, February 1991
*Greatest Hits II* released, November 1991
Freddie Mercury confirmed he had been tested HIV positive and had AIDS, 23 November 1991
Freddie died, 24 November 1991
Freddie's funeral, 27 November 1991
Tribute to Freddie Mercury concert, 20 April 1992
*Live at Wembley '86* released, June 1992

## PICTURE ACKNOWLEDGMENTS

Photographs reproduced by kind permission of London Features International;
Pictorial Press /Mazel, /Star File.

Front cover picture: London Features International

# INDEX

## A

Albums:
A Day at the Races ....................45
Flash Gordon ..................56, 58
The Game ................................56
Greatest Hits ..........................60
Innuendo ................................96
A Kind of Magic ......................79
Live Killers ..............................52
Live Magic ..............................79
The Freddie Mercury Album 110
The Miracle..............................87
News of the World............49,51
A Night at the Opera ...........38
Queen ....................................23
Queen II ................................26
Queen at The Beeb ................91
Sheer Heart Attack ................29
The Works ..............................66
America tour ......................28,32
Austin, Mary ..............................12

## B

Baker, Thomas, Roy ....................20
*Biggles* ......................................79
Bowie, David ..............................15

Brit Awards ................................48
Bulsara, Bomi ............................8
Bulsara, Jer ................................8

## C

Caballé, Montserrat ..................80
Capitol Records ..........................65
Clash (The) ................................47
Cross ..........................................81

## D

Damned (The)............................47
Deacon, John ............................12
De Lane Lea studio ....................20
Dobson, Anita ..........................78

## E

Earls Court ................................49

## F

First Queen UK tour ..................26
First Queen US tour ..................28
First world tour ........................48
Funeral ....................................104

## G

Grammy ....................................48
*Guinness Book of Records* ..........64

## H

*Highlander* ..........................78,79
Hunter, Ian ..............................44

Hyde Park ..................................44

## J

Jackson, Michael ......................70
Japan tour ................................35

## L

Live Aid ....................................74
Los Angeles ..............................28

## M

Magic Tour ................................79
May, Brian ................................10
May, Brian solo career ......65, 111
Melbourne (Australia) ..............27
Mercury, Freddie ........................8
Mercury, Freddie solo career ......65
*Metropolis* ................................68
Milton Keynes Bowl ..................64
Montreux Festival ......................68
Mott the Hoople ..................26, 28

## Q

Queen ......................................12
Queen Day ................................64

## R

Rock in Rio Festival ..................74

## S

Sao Paulo's Morumbi Stadium ...60
Sex Pistols ................................49

Smile ............................................ 10-11
**Songs:**
    Aerial Pursuit ............................ 79
    Another One Bites
        the Dust .............................. 57
    Backchat ...................................... 65
    Barcelona .................................... 80
    Bicycle Race ................................ 55
    Bohemian Rhapsody ...24,36,106
    Breakthru ..................................... 91
    Brighton Rock .............................. 29
    Chocks Away ............................... 79
    Crazy Little Thing
        Called Love ........................ 56
    Dancer ........................................ 63
    The Days of Our Lives ............. 106
    Death on Two Legs ................... 53
    Do You Want to be a Hero? ...79
    Fat Bottomed Girls ................... 55
    Flick of the Wrist ..................... 29
    Foolin' Around ........................... 75
    Friends Will Be Friends ............ 79
    Get Down, Make Love .....53, 55
    God Save the Queen ................ 53
    Good Old Fashioned
        Loverboy ............................ 47
    Great Pretender ......................... 80
    Hammer to Fall .......................... 74
    Heaven for Everyone ................ 81
    Headlong .................................... 96
    I Can't Live Without You ........ 96
    I'm Going Slightly Mad .......... 99

I'm in Love with My Car ......... 42
Innuendo ..................................... 95
The Invisible Man ...................... 91
It's Late ...................................... 52
I Want it All ............................... 88
I Want to Break Free ............... 67
Keep Yourself Alive .................. 24
Killer Queen ............................... 29
A Kind of Magic ........................ 77
Let's Turn It On ........................ 75
Living On My Own .................. 109
Love Kills .................................... 68
Love of My Life ......................... 55
The March of the Black
    Queen .................................... 24
Mr Bad Guy ............................... 75
My Fairy King ............................. 24
My Love is Dangerous .............. 75
The Night Comes Down ........... 20
No Turning Back ........................ 77
Now I'm Here ............................ 29
One Vision .................................. 76
The Prophet's Song ................... 41
Radio Ga Ga ............................... 66
Seven Seas of Rhye ................... 27
Sheer Heart Attack ................... 51
The Show Must Go On .............. 99
Sleeping on the Sidewalk ........ 52
Somebody to Love .................... 45
Spread Your Wings .................... 52
Thank God It's Christmas ........ 68
Tie Your Mother Down ............ 47

Time ............................................ 77
Under Pressure ................. 15, 60
We Are The Champions ......... 49
We Will Rock You ................... 51
    You're My Best Friend ............ 42
Staffell, Tim .............................. 10

**T**

Taking a break ........................... 64
Taylor, Roger .............................. 10
Taylor, Roger solo career ....63, 111
Tribute to Freddie Mercury ...... 107
Trident studio ............................. 20

**V**

Van Halen, Eddie ....................... 65
Vanilla Ice .................................. 95
Vicious, Sid ................................ 49

**W**

Washington ................................ 32

**Z**

Zanzibar ........................................ 8